Living With Power

3

[Jesus] "My grace is sufficient for you, for my power is made perfect in weakness." [Paul] "Therefore, I will boast all the more gladly about my weaknesses, so that Christ's power may rest on me."

2 CORINTHIANS 12:9

Operation Timothy

CBMC Publications

The Christian Business Men's Committee is an international evangelical organization of Christian business and professional men whose primary purpose is to present Jesus Christ as Savior and Lord to other business and professional men and to train these men to carry out the Great Commission.

CBMC of USA is a nondenominational, non-profit Christian ministry supported by gifts from people committed to reaching and discipling business and professional men for Jesus Christ.

More information may be obtained by writing:
    Christian Business Men's Committee of USA
    1800 McCallie Avenue
    Chattanooga, Tennessee 37404
    1-800-575-2262

Operation Timothy is an investigative Bible study with the goal of helping people to grow spiritually. It has been designed to serve as a link with the Living Proof I and II Video Series.

For more information, call 1-800-575-2262

Rob Suggs, *writer, cartoonist*

Isa Williams, *graphic designer*

Operation Timothy Workbook 3 – ISBN # 0-945292-03-1

Contents

APPOINTMENTS

Next Meeting _____ **Time** _____

_____

_____

_____

_____

Next Meeting _____ **Time** _____

_____

_____

_____

_____

Next Meeting _____ **Time** _____

_____

_____

_____

_____

Next Meeting _____ **Time** _____

_____

_____

_____

_____

Next Meeting _____ **Time** _____

_____

_____

_____

_____

Next Meeting _____ **Time** _____

_____

_____

_____

_____

Digging into the Bible

The Bible is the place where God comes from above and beyond the world to show Himself to His people. T.H. L. PARKER

It is the very nature and being of God to delight in communicating Himself. God has no selfishness. God keeps nothing to Himself. God's nature is to be always giving. ANDREW MURRAY

Men do not reject the Bible because it contradicts itself but because it contradicts them. E. PAUL HOVEY

WARM UP

"In Washington, in the Bureau of Standards, there is a platinum bar that is used as the standard meter for all measurements in the United States. It is 39.37 inches long. This bar is kept in a high vacuum at a constant temperature. An argument about the measurement of any object must be settled, ultimately, by comparison with the standard meter in Washington...God has given us His Word; it stands as the only infallible rule of faith and practice. Our lives are tested by its truth." DONALD GREY BARNHOUSE

THE BIG PICTURE.

I. What is the purpose of the Bible?
II. How does the Bible help me?
III. What will I do with the Bible?

I. WHAT IS THE PURPOSE OF THE BIBLE?

Take it from the Top. When we open our Bibles, it's easy to miss the significance: we're dealing with communication direct from the Creator of the Universe! Not only that — when we read it, this communication is applied specifically to our individual lives by His Spirit.

The Bible's place in our faith is critical. There's no way to understate the importance of understanding its authority. Review the "Bible at a Glance" chart in Book I, Chapter 1; you may also want to review that lesson to refresh your thinking about the Bible.

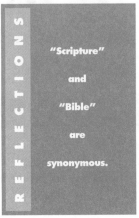

REFLECTIONS

"Scripture"

and

"Bible"

are

synonymous.

Read 2 Timothy 3:16.
How does this verse describe Scripture?

_____

Describe in your own words each of the four purposes of Scripture assigned here:

1 _____

2 _____

3 _____

4 _____

Describe the process of inspiration from God given in 2 Peter 1:20-21.

_____

_____

List five words which describe Scripture in Hebrews 4:12. Circle the one most meaningful to you, and explain why. _____

_____

_____

_____

II. How Does the Bible Help Me?

Using Psalm 19:7-11, complete this chart.

Verse	Bible is called...	Characteristics	What it does for me
7	Law	Perfect	Refreshes me spiritually
8	Statutes	Trustworthy	Gives me wisdom
9			
10			
11			

Word Pictures.
Look up each Scripture and write how the Word functions in that particular way.

JEREMIAH 23:29 _____

MATTHEW 4:4 _____

HEBREWS 4:12 _____

JAMES 1:23-25 _____

PSALM 119:105 _____

Count the Ways.

Match these verse references to the descriptions of what the Bible does for us as Christians.

JEREMIAH 15:16   Helps us grasp eternal life

JOHN 5:39   Keeps us from sin

2 PETER 1:4   Is a joy to consume

1 JOHN 2:1   Gives God's promises

The following chart comes from Psalm 119. This psalm deals with our attitudes and actions concerning Scripture. There are 176 verses in this chapter. All but six verses refer to Scripture, using the terms "law," "statutes," "precepts," "decrees," "commands," etc. Fill in the blanks, using verses 9-16.

Verse	Attitude	Action
9		Living by His Word
10	Seeking God with all our heart	Prayer for faithfulness
11		
12		
13		
14		
15		
16		

"This [Psalm 119] is both the longest psalm and the longest chapter in the Bible. It may have been written by Ezra after the Temple was rebuilt...as a repetitive meditation on the beauty of God's Word and how it helps us to stay pure and grow in faith. This psalm has 22 carefully constructed sections, each corresponding to a different letter in the Hebrew alphabet and each verse beginning with the letter of its section. Almost every verse mentions God's Word. Such repetition was common in the Hebrew culture. People did not have personal copies of the Scriptures to read as we do, so God's people memorized his Word and passed it along orally. The structure of this psalm allowed for easy memorization. Remember, God's Word, the Bible, is the only sure guide for living a pure life."

THE LIFE APPLICATION BIBLE, KJV, TYNDALE HOUSE PUBLISHERS, INC., WHEATON, IL, P.1052.

Based on Ezra 7:10, what three actions did Ezra take concerning Scripture?

_____

_____

What is significant about the sequence of the three? _____

_____

_____

_____

Just "brew" it. Read Colossians 3:16, in which Paul describes the process of being steeped in God's word, letting it "dwell in you richly." What specific ideas does he give, and what can you add to his list as ways to let the Word "brew" within you?

_____

_____

_____

Pick the two most important ideas above for yourself.
How can you practice them this week?

_____

_____

Get a grip. Here's a "hands on" approach to living and working with the Word of God.

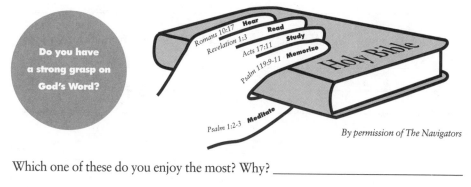

Do you have
a strong grasp on
God's Word?

Romans 10:17 Hear
Revelation 1:3 Read
Acts 17:11 Study
Psalm 119:9-11 Memorize
Psalm 1:2-3 Meditate

By permission of The Navigators

Which one of these do you enjoy the most? Why? _____

_____

Are you neglecting any? _____

_____

Hidden in a Safe Place. In Psalm 119:11, you found the concept of "hiding" God's Word in your heart. Scripture memorization is an essential tool for any Christian. With Bibles available and affordable for most people, why do you think it would be important to memorize verses?

_____

_____

_____

_____

Remember in Matthew 4:4, Jesus quoted Scripture to refute Satan.

The Holy Spirit, who dwells within us, loves to use Scripture. When we memorize a verse or passage, it's available to Him at a second's notice to guide us on the right path. How are you doing with the memory verses in the _Operation Timothy Series_?

_____

_____

Deep Thoughts. When we meditate on Scripture, we reflect on the verses in a prayerful spirit. We're seeking a deeper understanding, as well as the application of the verses to our lives. Our goal is to bring our lives closer to God's will by meditating on His Word.

Read Joshua 1:8. What does meditation help us do? _____

_____

What ultimate result in life does this verse predict for those who meditate on Scripture?

_____

_____

_____

III. WHAT WILL I DO WITH THE BIBLE?

Psalm 1 also deals with dwelling in God's Word. It provides an opportunity to meditate on and apply Scripture. There are several ways that you can do so with this or any passage in the Bible.

Read the Psalm carefully, exploring each verse. Read once for understanding, and read the verses a second time for application to your life.

Meditate on Psalm 1 or any verse or passage by asking yourself three questions:

1. WHAT? Observation What does it say?	2. SO WHAT? Personalization What does it say to me?	3. NOW WHAT? Application What will I do?
V.1 Man is blessed by not walking, standing, sitting with evil or evildoers	I need to choose carefully whom I will follow and spend time with and where I go	I will examine whom I am following and where I spend time to see if the influence is good or evil
V.2		
V.3		
V.4		
V.5		
V.6		

You might uses these questions as a guide for further meditation:

How is the Christian like a tree?

Compare godly and ungodly people in terms of habits, stability, and future.

What can you take from this psalm to help you build a better relationship with God?

_____

_____

 HEBREWS 4:12 "For the word of God is living and active. Sharper than any double-edged sword, it penetrates even to dividing soul and spirit, joints and marrow; it judges the thoughts and attitudes of the heart."

 The Gift that Keeps Giving. The Bible is an amazing, powerful gift from God. We have permanently at our fingertips the wisdom and perspective of the Creator of the universe. There is no area or crisis of life about which we can't draw guidance from the Bible. We need to be steeped in it — studying, meditating, applying — every day for the rest of our lives. For the Christian, it's as necessary and instinctive as breathing.

What has had the most significance for you in this chapter? _____

_____

_____

_____

_____

_____

_____

_____

"For the word
of God is living and
active. Sharper than
any double-edged
sword..."
HEBREWS 4:12

Scripture
Memory
Verse:

1 The Word of God NIV

2 TIMOTHY 3:16-17
All Scripture is God-breathed and is useful for teaching, rebuking, correcting and training in righteousness, so that the man of God may be thoroughly equipped for every good work.

2 TIMOTHY 3:16-17

NOTES

C H A P T E R   T W O

Communicating with God

Speech bubble: HE'S IN CONFERENCE WITH HIS SUPERVISOR; MAY I TAKE A MESSAGE?

That's What They Say:

Seven days without prayer makes one weak. ALLEN E. BARTLETT

I watched the deck stands on the great liner United States, *as they docked that ship in New York Harbor. Then inside the boat the great motors went to work and pulled on the great cable. But oddly enough, the pier wasn't pulled out to the ship; but the ship was pulled snugly up to the pier. Prayer is the rope that pulls God and man together. But it doesn't pull God down to us: it pulls us to Him.* BILLY GRAHAM

Can We Talk? Imagine a marriage without conversation. Each day, the husband returns from work and vegetates in front of the TV. In the morning, his wife sees only a newspaper obscuring his face. What chances do you give that marriage for success?

Like marriage, our relationship with God is dependent on communication. Fortunately, He has given us a two-way device by which we can transmit and receive signals, keeping in close contact. That device is called prayer.

Where Do Your Rate? Circle the selection below that best describes your prayer relationship with God:

a. He walks with me and He talks with me.
b. We check in daily.
c. We touch base from time to time.
d. I'm lousy at keeping in touch.
e. I've lost the address!
f. Other

W A R M U P

> "Look around and be distressed; look within and be depressed; look at Jesus and be at rest."
>
> CORRIE TEN BOOM

THE BIG PICTURE.

I. What are the essentials of prayer?
II. What are the benefits of prayer?
III. For whom do we pray?
IV. How do we spend time with God?

I. WHAT ARE THE ESSENTIALS OF PRAYER?

Why, When, and How. Recent studies indicate that most Americans believe in prayer. Everyone agrees that it is a wonderful thing. But many are unsure just how to go about it. Prayer, when do we start?

Why should we pray, according to Hebrews 4:16? And with what attitude?

_____

_____

When should we pray, according to 1 Thessalonians 5:17? _____

Practically, what does this mean? _____

_____

Psalm 62:8 agrees with that last verse, and adds a description of how we should pray. Restate that command in your own words. _____

_____

How about the *types* of prayer? Match the following five kinds of prayer with the verses that describe them. Try this as a "plan" next time you pray. In the margin to the right, you can jot a few notes applying each to your situation and feelings.

1 SAMUEL 12:23	Praise _____
PSALM 38:18	Thanksgiving _____
EPHESIANS 5:20	Confession _____
HEBREWS 13:15	Prayer for others' needs _____
JAMES 1:5	Prayer for our own needs _____

A Few Conditions. It's not enough to own an automobile. There are conditions that affect the quality of driving: gas, oil, water in the car, and air in the tires, for example. Then there are the road conditions to consider.

It's the same way with prayer. What conditions from the following verses affect or enhance our prayer?

PSALM 46:10	*ask in Jesus' name and you will receive, that your joy may be complete*
PSALM 66:18	*if we ask anything according to His will, He hears us & we know that we have what we asked of Him*
MATTHEW 21:22	*if you believe, you will receive whatever you ask for*
JOHN 15:7	*if I remain (abide) in Jesus and Jesus abides in me, I will receive whatever I ask*
JOHN 16:24	*if I cherish sin in my heart, God will not listen*
1 JOHN 5:14-15	*we ask & do not receive, because we ask with wrong motives, to spend on our own selfish desires*
JAMES 4:3	*be still, and know that I am God*

What about unanswered prayer? Everyone has prayed in some urgent circumstance, and failed to receive what they asked for. We tend to call this "unanswered prayer," but it's more accurate to say that the answer isn't the one we preferred. Little children ask for many things their parents think it unwise to give them. Our heavenly Parent, God, knows much better than we do what our needs are, and when they should be met. God answers every prayer — the mature Christian seeks to draw closer to Him to better understand those answers.

The Perfect Script. Jesus' friends once asked Him to teach them to pray. He gave us a model prayer, found in Matthew 6:9-13. Study that prayer carefully.

What are the God-centered requests? _____

_____

What are the personal requests? _____

_____

Why do you think Jesus used this order? _____

_____

In the space below, try rewriting Jesus' prayer using your own words, thoughts, and requests. _____

_____

_____

_____

_____

_____

_____

Filling in the Blanks. It's great to have "the script." But making the words come to life is another thing. How can we avoid dryness in our praying? How do we know what to pray for?

Who helps us pray, according to Romans 8:26, and how? _____

_____

What does Romans 8:5 have to do with our prayer? _____

_____

_____

II. WHAT ARE THE BENEFITS OF PRAYER?

A Job with Great Benefits. We pray out of our desire to know God better —
but that's only the beginning of the benefits that come to the believer through prayer.
The following verses will describe a few of those privileges.

What motivation to pray can we find in Jeremiah 33:3? _____

_____

According to Psalm 34:4, what does God do for us through prayer? _____

_____

Paul, the writer of Philippians, was a prisoner who knew the meaning of anxiety and
stress. In Philippians 4:6-7, what is his prescription? _____

_____

What can we expect when we pray this way? _____

_____

God knows everything already, of course. Why would He want us to pray about
"everything?" _____

_____

_____

_____

Reflect on one area in your own life about which you'd
like to experience this peace. Describe it below.

_____

_____

_____

_____

_____

_____

_____

REFLECTIONS

Prayer is indeed
a job with great
benefits. On the
other hand, we
can also say that
prayer is "not a
job — it's an
adventure!"

III. FOR WHOM DO I PRAY?

Praying for Others. When the Spirit gets involved, we understand His priorities and we find ourselves praying for others.

What special group does Paul pray for in Romans 10:1? _____

_____

What related subject for prayer is found in Matthew 9:37-38? _____

_____

Who else can you pray for, according to 1 Timothy 2:1-4? _____

_____

What kind of person does Luke 6:28 indicate we should pray for? _____

_____

This is tough! Why should we do it? _____

_____

Paul's beautiful, eloquent prayer in Ephesians 3:14-21 can be applied to people on your prayer list. In fact, praying Scripture back to God is a wonderful way to communicate with God. Why not take one name on your "Ten Most Wanted" card or prayer list and pray through Ephesians 3:14-21 for them.

Making a List and Checking it Twice. When your calendar is full of errands and appointments, you make a list. You can't afford to forget even one responsibility. Those we pray for are in no way less important. As you schedule a daily prayer time, have with you a prayer notebook in which you can jot requests. It will be before you as you pray. And you can also keep track of the answers to your prayer — that's the exciting part. Your prayer list might include some or all of the following:

Family members   Problem relationships
Non-Christian acquaintances   Governmental authorities
Pastor and church   Missionaries and Christian workers
Peers at work   Personal needs

Using your "10 Most Wanted" card is a good reminder to pray for those you personally want to reach with the good news of Christ. (Card in back of this book.)

TEN MOST-WANTED

1. _____
2. _____
3. _____
4. _____
5. _____
6. _____
7. _____
8. _____
9. _____
10. _____

I will faithfully pray for the salvation of the above and will attempt to reach them for Christ through personal witness and various outreach efforts.

"The earnest prayer of a righteous man has great effect." JAMES 5:16

Sample:
Prayer Requests List:

Date	Request	Answer (Date)
_____	_____	_____
_____	_____	_____
_____	_____	_____
_____	_____	_____
_____	_____	_____

Too Busy Not to Pray. We've all said this: "Prayer is wonderful. I just have trouble finding the time." The truth is this: we always find time for the things we find most important. Our hearts prioritize our agendas. In Luke 10:38-42, study the contrasting agendas of two women, Mary and Martha. Write your observations about their activities below.

Mary   **Martha**

_____

_____

_____

_____

How did Jesus respond to these two approaches? _____

_____

List the activities most likely to distract you from spending time with God.

_____

_____

_____

What can you do specifically to overcome some of these distractions?

_____

_____

What is the most exciting new truth you've learned in this session? What is the greatest change you expect to make in your prayer life? _____

_____

_____

_____

_____

_____

_____

_____

IV. HOW DO WE SPEND TIME WITH GOD?

Quiet Time

Much has been written, suggested and outlined for believers to have a fruitful and effective quiet time. These quiet times have truly been daily spiritual food for many, yet many others have felt guilty or somehow inferior for their inconsistency. Our focus is not to put a burden and weight to go through some daily ritual, but to deepen our intimacy with God.

So why have a quiet time?
What is a quiet time?
When and how can I have a quiet time?

Why have a quiet time?

David, in Psalm 27:8, says "My heart says of you, 'Seek his face!' Your face, LORD, I will seek." God called David to seek His face. God desires our presence — much like a father desires to be with his children. This is our motivation to be with God — He wants us!

A quiet time is time with our Lord — to hear from Him, to call out to Him, to be with Him. David expresses his heart to be with God in Psalm 27:4, "One thing I ask of the Lord, this is what I seek: that I may dwell in the house of the Lord all the days of my life, to gaze upon the beauty (delightfulness) of the Lord and to seek him in his temple." David wanted one thing of God — to be with God, to know and love God, to consider His ways. This was his heart's desire — a yearning, a thirst. It was his highest priority. The psalmist in Psalm 42:1 illustrates this: "As the deer pants for streams of water, so my soul pants for you, O God."

What is a quiet time?

- A special time to meditate and reflect on God's Word
    for inspiration
    guidance
    hope
- A time to hear from God
    Jeremiah 33:3 "Call to Me and I will answer you and tell you great and
    unsearchable things you do not know."
- A time to pray for the lost (10 Most Wanted)
- A time to call upon God in prayer

Many Christians have found the letters ACTS helpful in praying. The letters stand for Adoration, Confession, Thanksgiving, and Supplication (requests). This is a sensible sequence: we get everything in perspective by adoring, or praising, God for who He is. This reveals our own inadequacies and failures, and we confess them. As we do this, we know God forgives us, and as we feel a refreshing sense of thanksgiving, we begin to express our gratitude for His many blessings. Finally, with the Spirit's assistance, we can properly ask Him to supply our needs and the needs of others.

ACTS is NOT a list of "to do's." It is a guideline to help focus our prayers.

When?

Whenever you so desire! Many have found it beneficial early in the morning, before they engage in daily activities. Many of the psalms encourage this. Others have found that night time may be more suitable for them. Any time is good — as long as you take time to do so. Yet, don't feel guilty if you miss this time. Consistency comes with growth, practice, and maturity.

How?

Ten to fifteen minutes may be a realistic time period with which to begin. You may desire to lengthen this time eventually. You might spend it in the following way:

> 5 minutes of prayer
> 5 minutes of Bible reading
> 5 minutes of reflection/meditation

Find a quiet place, free from distractions. You may want to be at a table or desk in order to be able to write and reflect.

Some practical suggestions to get started:

You can read through the Psalms in a month by reading 5 psalms a day. You can also read through Proverbs in a month, one chapter a day. Several Bibles are available that are designed to help you read through the Bible in a year. This usually takes only about 15-20 minutes a day of reading. *The Daily Walk Bible* published by Walk Thru the Bible Ministries, is available in several translations and gives an overview of the day's reading, insight into some of the history and other background, and helps in applying Scripture to daily life.

 Do you currently have a plan for spending time with God? If not, what will you do to begin? _____

_____

_____

_____

_____

_____

Scripture Memory Verse:

2 Assurance of Answered Prayer   NIV

PHILIPPIANS 4:6-7

Do not be anxious about anything, but in everything, by prayer and petition, with thanksgiving, present your requests to God. And the peace of God, which transcends all understanding, will guard your hearts and your minds in Christ Jesus.

PHILIPPIANS 4:6-7

NOTES

REFLECTIONS

"Being hurried comes naturally; while being at rest requires an ongoing appraisal of priorities. All of us who are serious about our spiritual life and our family life must counter the forces threatening our ability to maintain rest."

TIM KIMMEL,
SURVIVING LIFE IN THE FAST LANE

3 Thriving in the Church

Unless you've recently sliced Matthew 16:18 out of your Bible, it still says the same thing Jesus said. It still includes an unconditional promise that the church is His personal project ('I will build __my__ church') and also that it will be perpetually invincible. No way will 'the gates of hell' put it out of business. When you chew on that thought long enough, you begin to realize that the church is the impervious anvil, and all these other hot items, no matter how impressive and loud and intimidating, will ultimately cool off and be replaced. CHARLES SWINDOLL

Living Proof I, Evangelism Video Series ©1990 (CBMC and Navpress) tells the story of Gerry and Linda Sanders, a married couple with a teenage son. Through their neighbors, the Warners, and a neighborhood study of John's Gospel, the Sanders come to receive Jesus Christ as their personal Savior and Lord. They have no background of church involvement or membership, but now Gerry realizes his family's need. He and Linda want to know how to go about finding where they can worship.

What would you tell them? _____

_____

What has been your experience with church?

_____

_____

_____

_____

_____

W A R M U P

THE BIG PICTURE.

There is plenty of confusion about the church today. Let's see exactly what the Scriptures have to say.
In this chapter we will discuss four issues:

I. What is the church?
II. What does the church do?
III. Should I be involved in the church?
IV. How can I thrive in the church?

I. WHAT IS THE CHURCH?

In Search of the Church.

They come in all shapes and sizes, styles of architecture, denominations, reputations, social stances, and it seems as if there's one on every block. The music varies; the dress codes differ. What is this thing called "the church" all about? Because the term "church" is used in different ways to denote different meanings, new Christians are often confused when these are used interchangeably. The Greek word for "church" in the New Testament refers to all believers who make up the body of Christ. However, Christians also use this term to indicate the local group with whom they choose to worship and grow spiritually. They also often use the word "church" to indicate the physical building or property. Just as we, as individuals, are part of a local group, so the local group and all the individual believers are a part of the larger body of Christ.

How is the church described in 1 Timothy 3:15? _____

_____

According to Matthew 16:18, is the church a building? Explain. _____

_____

_____

Who is the leader of the church, according to Ephesians 5:23? What reason is given?

_____

_____

How is the church described in Ephesians 1:22-23? _____

_____

How does one get into the church from 1 Corinthians 12:11-14 and Romans 8:9?

_____

When does this happen? _____

_____

In your own words, summarize "what is the church?" _____

_____

_____

_____

Under Construction. Another important passage about the church is found in Ephesians 2:19-22. In verses 20-22, match the "building materials" with the spiritual content.

The bricks   God's Spirit _____

_____

Foundation   Christ _____

_____

The cornerstone People _____

_____

The occupant   The Bible (apostles and prophets) _____

In the right margin above, note how each of these fits the analogy (comparison).

Have you ever thought of yourself as a building project? According to Ephesians, in the church we're being "built together." And when the Spirit comes to inhabit the premises, we become more than the sum of our parts.

Big or Small? How large must a body of believers be to call itself a church? Read Matthew 18:20. _____

_____

Again, the church is not a building; it's believers blessed by God's presence.

The Greek word used in Scripture for "church" means a "called out" group, or "assembly." In the next section, we'll discover just what the church is called out to do.

WHICH DENOMINATION IS THE TRUE CHURCH?

For new Christians, denominations can be puzzling. Not only is God's church divided and sub-divided, even within the divisions there are differences. Denominations, of course, are not found in the Bible — they have been superimposed over the ages by Christians, generally divided by doctrinal interpretation. And some churches are independent; that is, they belong to no denomination or governing body.

No one denomination can demonstrate it's the only true church.

When sorting through the denominational maze, be sure to ask your Operation Timothy Leader for help. Ask a pastor for literature about his denomination's doctrine. Most will be happy to help you and answer your questions. Also, see the section on "Identifying a Thriving Church" in this chapter which will help you with specific questions to use during your investigation.

II. WHAT DOES THE CHURCH DO?

No Place for "Pew Potatoes." Many people think of the church as a quiet place to hear sacred music of bygone eras, and perhaps listen to an encouraging sermon. The Bible's job description of the church is a bit more exciting.

Read Acts 2:42-47. This describes the first believers, gathered together after Jesus' ascension from earth. In verse 42, what are some of the activities described?

_____

_____

In verse 47, what results are described? _____

_____

According to Matthew 28:18-20, what is the church called out to do?

_____

Jesus described His purpose, for us to carry on, in Luke 19:10. What is it?

_____

Pardon, We're Expanding.

The church, then, has received the blueprint. It's not so much a place to come to as a place to go from. When Jesus said He would build His church, He intended to keep building until it was a great enough structure for everyone. The church is His construction crew.

The "One Anothers."

The New Testament offers a series of "one another" statements that describe our ministry through the church to each other. Fill in the "one anothers:"

ROMANS 15:7 _____

GALATIANS 5:13 _____

GALATIANS 6:2 _____

EPHESIANS 4:2 _____

EPHESIANS 5:21 _____

PHILIPPIANS 2:3-4 _____

COLOSSIANS 3:16 _____

1 THESSALONIANS 4:18 _____

1 JOHN 4:7 _____

The church reaches outward to lost people, and inward to embrace its own.

> Another dimension of this truth is community. The body "builds itself up in love." Koinonia, as used for example by John, means "life in the family." Body life is twenty-four hours a day, seven days a week, and embraces the full spectrum of our activities. As we go through life as believers, we are to attentively serve one another, encouraging one another toward godliness in every area. As believers formed themselves into identifiable bodies in the first centuries, their times of gathering were just the tip of the iceberg of their life together.
>
> Our life as a family in God's household is critical to our going to the world. As we have previously observed, it is the unique nature of this life together that makes us light in the world. Then, as we allow ourselves to be scattered into the world, our need for one another becomes a matter of life and death. We will need like never before the care and support of our brothers and sisters.
>
> Jim Petersen, *Lifestyle Discipleship*, page 172

III. SHOULD I BE INVOLVED IN THE CHURCH?

No Lone Rangers. We have Christ. We have the indwelling Spirit, and in the Bible we have God's Word. Can't one be a good Christian without involvement with others?

That idea is foreign to the New Testament, most of whose books are written to groups of people rather than individuals. The key understanding is Paul's metaphor: the church is Christ's body.

How does 1 Corinthians 12:27 answer this section's question? _____

_____

_____

_____

Read 1 Corinthians 12:12-26. What is Paul's central point in this passage? _____

_____

_____

_____

In what way do you think Christians in a church function as a kind of body? _____

_____

_____

_____

In Ephesians 5:31,32, Paul refers to a "profound mystery," comparing two things. What are they? _____

_____

How does this affect your thinking about marriage? About the church?

_____

_____

Wouldn't it be wonderful to be part of this type of local church?

We see, then, that for those who take the Bible seriously, involvement together with other believers is a given. The church is the way Christ lives and works in the world, and the subtraction of any individual diminishes the whole — as well as the individual. We need each other, we need Christ, and Christ has chosen to live in and work through us.

We've defined the church, and taken a look at its task. We've discovered that every Christian should be involved. One question remains: How can we get the most from this involvement?

IV. HOW CAN I THRIVE IN THE CHURCH?

Everyone's heard the one about "all the hypocrites in the church." And nobody wants to fall into that trap. It's easy to imagine just what the church *could* be — all it takes is to study the New Testament church! The body of Christ will thrive when its members begin to thrive within it.

Read 2 Timothy 4:2-5. What is the major emphasis for the church's duty in this passage?

_____

_____

In 1 Corinthians 14:12, which spiritual gifts should we seek? _____

_____

What attitude toward the church is described in Acts 20:28? _____

_____

Read Hebrews 10:24-25. What "one another" action is set out? _____

_____

What failure is warned against in this passage? _____

_____

CARING FOR YOUR BODY

The Bible, then, teaches us to maintain sound doctrine; to use our gifts to build the Body, protecting and shepherding the believers; to constantly encourage each other to be everything we can be; and to be committed and faithful to Christ. The Christian who does these things will never be a hypocrite! He or she will thrive not only in the church, but in life itself.

Identifying a Thriving Church

Even if you're clear on the denominational issue, it's still likely your local yellow pages are filled with churches. How can you identify whether one is right for you and your family?

First, if you are currently in a local church or assembly, look at this group through the lens of Scripture that you have just studied above. Talk over your questions with your Timothy leader. Ask where he goes to church and why he is attending there. If you are looking for a church home, visit several churches that believers you trust recommend. Don't make your decision strictly on the quality of the preaching or the worship service elements. Check on the types of activities and ministries in that fellowship. Is there an active Bible study ministry? Are members involved in evangelism? Is there dynamic, in-depth ministry to meet the needs of your whole family (your spouse, your children, etc.)? Is the church effective in ministering to the needs of its community? If you're liking what you see, make an appointment to talk to the pastor or a staff member. Ask him about his church's doctrinal stance. Look for an evangelical pastor who supports the infallibility of Scripture; the full deity of Christ, and His humanity, sinlessness, resurrection, return and the "born again" life and ministry of the believer. These should all be "givens" in a New Testament fellowship. Be cautious if the elder or pastor is non-committal on these basics.

> **ABSOLUTE BASICS IN ANY ASSEMBLY OR CHURCH:**
>
> 1. They believe the Bible from cover to cover.
> 2. They believe the virgin birth of Christ.
> 3. Christ is fully man and fully God, lived a sinless life, and after 33 years was crucified.
> 4. Christ rose from the dead (bodily resurrection), ascended into heaven and is coming again.
> 5. The church is Christ's body.

Caution: Go slowly in making decisions in this area, particularly if your family is already involved in a local congregation. Pray, discuss thoroughly with your spouse and children. Ask counsel from your Timothy Leader before taking any action steps. There are many factors to consider, and your Leader will be able to help you consider and weigh these.

What new insights did you gain or what questions surfaced as a result of this lesson? _____

_____

_____

_____

*Scripture
Memory
Verse:*

3 Christ and the Church   NIV

COLOSSIANS 1:18
And he is the head of the body, the church; he is the beginning and the firstborn from among the dead, so that in everything he might have the supremacy.

COLOSSIANS 1:18

NOTES

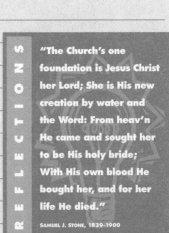

4 Becoming a Person of Character

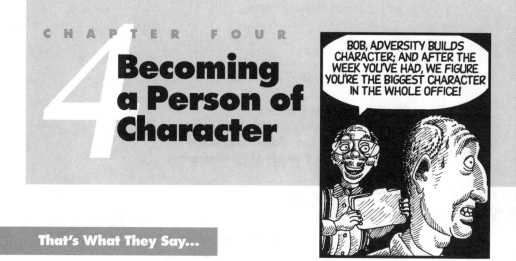

BOB, ADVERSITY BUILDS CHARACTER; AND AFTER THE WEEK YOU'VE HAD, WE FIGURE YOU'RE THE BIGGEST CHARACTER IN THE WHOLE OFFICE!

That's What They Say...

Man will do in the presence of God what he will never do in the presence of men.
WALT HENRICHSEN, BIBLE TEACHER

People need to see the gospel lived out in us if they are going to understand what it really is that we have to offer. If the quality of character is not there, the best knowledge and skills become meaningless. Our TV evangelists have the knowledge and they have honed their skills to an art form, but the notorious flaws in character of some turn it all to straw. JIM PETERSEN, NAVIGATORS

Have patience! God isn't through with me yet. BUMPER STICKER

Character is what a man is in the dark. DWIGHT L. MOODY

Reflect: How do you react to the quote: "Character is what a man is in the dark?"

_____

_____

_____

WARM UP

It's a fast-food, quick gratification world. We want to lose weight this week, and earn a fortune this year. We want it, and we want it *now*.

But some things can't be attained overnight. One of them is character. God wants to build in us strong character, with clear values and unflinching integrity. But the old self must be replaced with the new child — and no child grows up overnight.

THE BIG PICTURE.

In this chapter, we will discuss four areas:

     I. What is character?
     II. Why God develops character
     III. How God develops character
     IV. My role in developing character

I. WHAT IS CHARACTER?

Character is defined by the dictionary as "moral or ethical strength". Let's look at some Biblical pictures of the moral strength we call character.

Read carefully the list of attributes found in Galatians 5:22-23. Which do you respect the most? Why? _____

_____

_____

_____

Which is most difficult for you? _____

_____

According to verse 22, what is the source of the character defined by these? _____

_____

What is a basic measuring stick for character, according to 1 John 5:2-3? _____

_____

The following verses describe aspects of Christian character. Identify each aspect by underlining and writing a one or two word answer to identify the character quality (or qualities).

1 CORINTHIANS 15:58 "Therefore, my dear brothers, stand firm. Let nothing move you. Always give yourselves fully to the work of the Lord, because you know that your labor is not in vain." _____

1 THESSALONIANS 5:8 "Give thanks in all circumstances, for this is God's will for you in Christ Jesus." _____

JAMES 2:8 "If you really keep the royal law found in Scripture, 'Love your neighbor as yourself,' you are doing right." _____

ROMANS 13:8 "Let no debt remain outstanding, except the continuing debt to love one another, for he who loves his fellowman has fulfilled the law."

_____

MATTHEW 7:12 "So in everything, do to others what you would have them do to you..." _____

COLOSSIANS 3:13 "Bear with each other and forgive whatever grievances you may have against one another." _____

1 PETER 5:5 "Young men, in the same way be submissive to those who are older. All of you, clothe yourselves with humility toward one another, because, 'God opposes the proud but gives grace to the humble.'" _____

MATTHEW 5:8 "Blessed are the pure in heart, for they will see God." _____

1 CORINTHIANS 6:20 "You were bought at a price. Therefore honor God with your body." _____

HEBREWS 12:14 "Make every effort to live in peace with all men and to be holy; without holiness no one will see the Lord." _____

2 CORINTHIANS 9:7 "Each man should give what he has decided in his heart to give, not reluctantly or under compulsion, for God loves a cheerful giver."

_____

PROVERBS 19:11: "A man's wisdom gives him patience; it is to his glory to overlook an offense." _____

We've barely tapped the surface of the Bible's teaching on character. Yet we see a clear picture of the kind of person God desires us to become. Why is the molding of character so important to God?

In 2 Peter 1:3-9, what are we to add to our faith? _____

_____

In verse 3, whose power is the resource for doing this? _____

In verses 9, 10, what are the results? _____

II. WHY GOD DEVELOPS CHARACTER

Testing, testing. The first recorded test of human character is found in Genesis 2 and 3. As soon as He created them, God defined limits for Adam and Eve — a command to keep. They failed that test. But God has never given up on us. He continues to build into our lives the structures and limits that mold character within us.

What clue to God's desire for strong character in us is found in Genesis 1:27? _____

_____

What is God's basic approach toward us according to Jeremiah 31:3? _____

_____

In Philippians 3:13-14, how does Paul view God's ultimate plan for him? _____

_____

_____

_____

"Let go, Let God"

Romans 5:1-5 describes the process of character development.
Where does character come from? _____

_____

What is the result of character development? _____

_____

How does Romans 12:1-2 describe the process of building character? _____

_____

_____

This passage describes character-building as (circle one):

1. reformation,
2. conformation,
3. transformation.

What do you think the difference is? _____

_____

_____

What will this process enable us to do? _____

_____

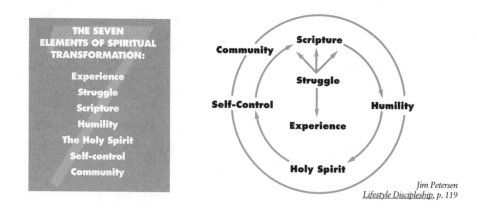

THE SEVEN
ELEMENTS OF SPIRITUAL
TRANSFORMATION:

Experience
Struggle
Scripture
Humility
The Holy Spirit
Self-control
Community

Jim Petersen
Lifestyle Discipleship, p. 119

What else can mature Christians do, according to Romans 15:1-2? _____

_____

The Visionary Sculptor.

It is said that Michelangelo, the artist, visited a quarry looking for the perfect marble. He found a block that was profoundly flawed; yet he took it. He later said that when he looked at the stone he saw the angel it could become. His task was to liberate the angel from the marble, by removing "everything that is not the angel."

God sees our flaws. But He sees Himself in us, too, and character-building is His constant chiseling away of everything ungodly.

III. HOW GOD DEVELOPS CHARACTER

Dave Dravecky, All-Star baseball pitcher, lost his left arm at the very peak of his career. He told *USA Today,* "I've come to understand that God is really shaping and molding my character. I've come to realize that real growth of character takes place in the valleys of life."

What pain have you experienced and/or are you experiencing? _____

_____

_____

_____

_____

_____

What startling statement does Romans 8:28 make about the nature of all our experiences? _____

_____

To whom does this apply? _____

How should this truth affect the way you view daily life? _____

_____

_____

Read Hebrews 12:7-11. How does this passage define hardship? _____

_____

_____

_____

In what way did discipline affect your upbringing? _____

_____

The word *discipline* comes from the word *disciple* which means a devoted student.

_____

_____

_____

Read James 1: 2-4. What attitude should we have about trials?

_____

Based on vv. 3-4, fill in: the _____ of your faith
develops _____ .

_____ must finish its work
so that you may be _____ and _____ .

In what ways do you find this to be true? _____

_____

_____

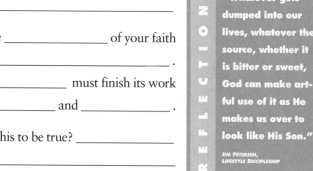

REFLECTIONS

"Whatever gets
dumped into our
lives, whatever the
source, whether it
is bitter or sweet,
God can make art-
ful use of it as He
makes us over to
look like His Son."

JIM PETERSEN,
LIFESTYLE DISCIPLESHIP

What advice can we take from James 5:10-11 to be encouraged in suffering? _____

_____

As Philippians chapter 2 tells us, Christ faced a brutal death because it was the only
doorway to the destiny God planned for Him and us. Similarly, He allows us to suffer
because it sculpts us into the new creatures He wants us to be.

Based on the Scripture passages studied in this section, what should be our attitude
toward suffering? We will delve into this in more depth in the next chapter. _____

_____

IV. MY ROLE IN DEVELOPING CHARACTER

"The outcome
of your life will be
determined by
your character"

Character is one's moral strength or excellence. It is the fortitude
one has in the face of contrary influences.

As we have seen, God promises to develop our character as we
respond to difficulties with hope, perseverance, and the attitude of learning to patiently
endure and learn from our brokenness. In fact, suffering itself helps produce these
responses as we yield to God and cry out to Him in dependence and powerlessness.

Read Hebrews 11:32-40. It describes God's people who had been faithful — even to
the point of not seeing their hopes fulfilled. Describe their attitude and circumstances.

_____

_____

_____

How do you react to this? _____

_____

Hebrews 12:1-4 continues this train of thought. How are we to respond to situations that build our character? _____

_____

_____

_____

What key principle is given in Colossians. 2:6,7? _____

_____

How Do I Gain This Character?

Character is shaped by:

GOD   **MY CHOICES**   **OTHERS.**

God at Work:

God's greatest desire is to prepare us for an eternity with Him. He utilizes His supernatural power, circumstances and people in this character-building process.

Examine Romans 5:3-5. What is the process to develop proven character? _____

_____

Why does God discipline us? Hebrews 12:10,11. _____

_____

Has God operated in your life in this manner? How? _____

_____

At the heart of perseverance or patience is a choice that I make. What is that choice and how does it relate to character? _____

_____

_____

Can we develop character by the "Self-improvement Plan" or "You *Can* Develop Godly Character in Three Easy Lessons"? What does Galatians 5:22,23 and John 15:5 say about the power source for character development? _____

_____

_____

_____

Another principle of character development is the "time" perspective. If we focus on a 70 year time span, then our tendency is to panic, become fearful; but if we look through the lens of an eternal perspective — 200, 300, 1,000 years from now — it helps us put present problems and experiences in perspective and realize that God is working with the eternal in view for us.

Perseverance or patience literally means "to bear up under"

Living Proof II, Discipleship Video Series, Sessions 10 & 12, dramatize this process of character development through the lives of the actors, particularly "Bill." You can see the 70-year plan vs. the eternal plan illustrated.

A Look Within:

In the development of character, God calls us to examine ourselves on the inside. My true character is reflected in my thoughts and attitudes (my values). In this diagram, my character begins with my world view, or in other words, my view of God. My character is reflected in my values and finally displayed in my behavior.

World View

Values

Behavior

Read Matthew 5:1-11, 27-28. Look at the Sermon on the Mount in Matthew 5:1-11. In both cases, Jesus begins with an existing standard and looks deeper, beneath the surface. What reveals Jesus' concern with attitude as well as action in these verses?

_____

_____

_____

_____

Issues of honesty, integrity, and humility are at the heart of our character or moral excellence.

Restate Proverbs 26:24 in your own words. _____

_____

_____

"If you tell the truth, you don't have to remember anything."

MARK TWAIN

Do you _____ agree _____ disagree with the following statement:

"Many people cut corners on so-called 'little' things such as telling half-truths, taking office supplies home, stretching the expense account, fudging on taxes or thinking impure thoughts."

What is an area of your life in which you struggle with being completely honest?

_____

_____

How have you attempted to deal with this in the past? _____

_____

_____

_____

If you feel defeated from past or current efforts in this area, you may need to look deeper at some underlying root issues that may be hindering you, such as fear of rejection, fear of failure, anger at God, bitterness, etc. Spend some time reflecting on and allowing God to examine your heart in these areas. Confess anything God reveals and ask for God's mercy and guidance in how to deal with these.

What principle is found in Luke 16:10 as it relates to character? _____

_____

Integrity — once lost — is nearly impossible to regain.

The Help of Another:

In developing character, a third help is enlisting the assistance of others who will hold you accountable for your actions and attitudes, particularly ones with which you struggle.

Pat Morley, in *Man in the Mirror*, defines accountability: "To be regularly answerable for each of the key areas of our lives to qualified people."

What are some of these key areas?

Time
with God
with our spouse
with our children

Integrity
in finances
in work
in friendships

Who are these "qualified" people? Someone who has
a heart for God
a heart to help others
the ability to speak the truth honestly, yet lovingly

What does Proverbs 27:17 say about this accountability? _____
_____

Do you have someone who helps you to stay accountable? Someone who will ask you the tough questions? Why, why not? _____
_____

List two reasons why we find this kind of relationship difficult. _____
_____

According to Jeremiah 17:9, why do we need accountability? _____
_____
_____

Accountability here and now is important because God will ultimately hold us accountable for all that we say and do.

React to this statement: "Some men have spectacular failures where in an instant they abruptly burst into flames, crash, and burn. But the more common way men get into trouble evolves from hundreds of tiny decisions — decisions which go undetected — that slowly, like water tapping on a rock, wear down man's character. Not blatantly or precipitously, but subtly, over time, we get caught in a web of cutting corners and compromise, self-deceit and wrong thinking, which goes unchallenged by anyone in our lives." _____

_____

_____

_____

_____

_____

Living Above Mediocrity. Try though it may to pull us down, the world will fail when it comes to the people of God. God has special things planned for us. He wants us to be uncompromising in integrity; mature in wisdom; overflowing in love; unforgettable in character — in short, the very image of Jesus Christ. As the Father sculpts us, the chisel can be painful; but the goal of Christ's likeness makes it all worth it. And as we begin to change, the world changes, too.

"I'm not saying that I have this all together, that I have it made. But I am well on my way, reaching out for Christ, who has so wondrously reached out for me. Friends, don't get me wrong: By no means do I count myself an expert in all of this, but I've got my eye on the goal, where God is beckoning us onward — to Jesus. I'm off and running, and I'm not turning back."

PHILIPPIANS 3:12-14,
IN EUGENE PETERSON'S PARAPHRASE, THE MESSAGE

Are you willing to enter into an accountable relationship? _____

With whom? Consider some of the relationships you currently have. You may want to ask someone to be of help to you in this area. _____

_____

In which area of your character have you seen growth, change, progress? How?

_____

_____

On what area is God currently working to transform you into His likeness? How?

_____

_____

Scripture Memory Verse:

4 Transformed, not conformed   NIV

ROMANS 12:1-2

Therefore, I urge you, brothers, in view of God's mercy, to offer your bodies as living sacrifices, holy and pleasing to God — this is your spiritual act of worship. Do not conform any longer to the pattern of this world, but be transformed by the renewing of your mind. Then you will be able to test and approve what God's will is — his good, pleasing and perfect will.

ROMANS 12:1-2

NOTES

REFLECTIONS

"We take excellent care of our bodies, which we have for only a lifetime; yet we let our souls shrivel, which we will have for eternity."

BILLY GRAHAM

5 Pursuing Intimacy with God

...SO TUESDAY IS OUT, TOO, LORD; WEDNESDAY IS GOLF. I TRY TO KEEP THURSDAY OPEN, AND WEEKENDS ARE SIMPLY OUT OF THE QUESTION. SAY, I CAN FIT YOU IN FOR MONDAY COFFEE BREAK!

DAY TIMER

That's What They Say:

You come to realize as you listen that God is actually opening his heart to you, making friends with you and enlisting you as a colleague — ... a covenant partner. It is a staggering thing, but it is true — the relationship in which sinful human beings know God is one in which God, so to speak, takes them onto his staff, to be henceforth his fellow workers and personal friends. J. I. PACKER IN KNOWING GOD

You will never be satisfied just to know about God. Really knowing God only comes through experience as He reveals Himself to you. HENRY BLACKABY IN EXPERIENCING GOD

Most Christians seek to enlist God to solve their problems; what God wants is for Christians to use their problems to develop deeper intimacy with Him. DR. LARRY CRABB

WARM UP

Do you believe in God? Ultimately, that's actually not the significant question. Surveys show most Americans believe in God even though crime increases, immorality runs rampant, and church attendance drops.
Let's ask the question another way:
What do you believe *about* God? J. B. Phillips' classic book, *Your God is Too Small*, catalogues the various inadequate images most people carry of their Creator. We must know God as He is, but even more — we must know Him *intimately.*

THE BIG PICTURE.

In this chapter, we'll discuss four issues concerning the pursuit of intimacy with God:

> I. Who is God?
> II. How does God pursue us?
> III. How can we grow in intimacy with God?
> IV. How can we find God in our suffering?

I. WHO IS GOD?

How old is God? (Psalm 93:2) _____

_____

Where can God be found? (Psalm 139:7-8) _____

_____

Describe God's power. (Isaiah 40:26-28) _____

_____

Describe God's determination. (Isaiah 46:10) _____

_____

What does creation reveal about God? (Romans 1:18-20) _____

_____

To what extent is God interested in us? (Psalm 139:1-2) _____

_____

What is God's relation to evil? (Psalm 5:4-6) _____

_____

How is God described? (Hebrews 12:28) _____

_____

What does this verse say God is? (1 John 4:8) _____

_____

> "What we believe about God is the most important thing about us."
>
> A. W. TOZER

Henry Blackaby's, *Experiencing God*, lists over 360 names for God which reveal His awesome character. A few are listed below.

Father	Jesus	Holy Spirit
Creator of heaven and earth	Alpha and Omega	Counselor
Eternal King	Chief Shepherd	Breath of the Almighty
Father of compassion	Cornerstone	Spirit of Christ
Father to the fatherless	Faithful and True	Comforter
I AM	King of Kings	Spirit of holiness
LORD who is there	Lamb of God	Spirit of wisdom
LORD will provide	The Word	Spirit of truth
Majesty	Mediator	Voice of the LORD

II. HOW DOES GOD PURSUE US?

"The Hound of Heaven" — that's the name of a classic poem about the God who relentlessly pursues us. As we've seen, He's eternal, infinite, all-powerful, all-knowing, morally perfect; yet He chooses to know, and love, and be known by His imperfect, finite children. How does He bridge the tremendous chasm which separates us?

Do we naturally seek Him? Why or why not? (Psalms 14:1-3, Romans 3:10-11)

_____

_____

_____

_____

What is the "fuel" for His pursuit of us? (Jeremiah 31:3) _____

_____

How does God pursue us? (1 John 4:9-10) _____

_____

Does God make it difficult to know Him? Why or why not? (Revelation 3:20)

_____

_____

What provision does God make when we sin? (1 John 1:8,9) _____

_____

New Occupant. How does God then make intimacy with us possible?

EZEKIEL 36:26-27 _____

_____

Did you know.....? 1 CORINTHIANS 3:16 _____

_____

Describe the Spirit's work within us. ROMANS 8:26,27 _____

_____

In a Nutshell. It's an astounding fact that not only does He desire for us to know Him intimately — He takes the initiative. "You did not choose me, but I chose you," says Jesus in John 15:16. He became one of us, the only possible way to bridge the absolute chasm between us. And He demonstrated His love by dying for us. Because He's cleansed us, He can live within us. God has pursued us, and "caught" us. (John 12:32)

III. HOW CAN WE GROW IN INTIMACY WITH GOD?

The Christian life is not one of the status quo in which we enter into a relationship with God and just stay there. Although some people do stagnate, God's desire is that we grow. A relationship with God is the foundation upon which we then grow in our fellowship with God resulting in intimacy with Him. It is a life-long process — we don't just arrive. Much like a marriage, we can grow more deeply in love with our Lord over time and through experiences.

What is the process? Is it something I *do*?

This spiritual growth or transformation begins with God's pursuit of me. He pursues me to establish a relationship. He continues to pursue me to develop intimacy. We have just examined these two ideas in this chapter. God initiates by using circumstances, struggles and trials to reveal Himself and His character. As I find myself in the presence of God, my view of Him and my view of who I am (a sinful man) become apparent to me!

How did each of these men react in the presence of God?

JOHN   REVELATION 1:17 _____

_____

PAUL   ACTS 26:13-15 _____

_____

EZEKIEL   EZEKIEL 1:28 _____

_____

_____

ISAIAH   ISAIAH 6:5-8 _____

_____

_____

> This reaction is a part of what the Bible calls the "fear of God". Psalm 25:14 states that "The Lord confides in those who fear him..." Fearing God is both a reverential awe of God, as well as an acknowledgement of His justice and power.

Why do you think "intimacy with God" is connected to "the fear of God"?

_____

_____

_____

The men listed above were humbled by coming into the presence of God. When we are humble and broken, God meets us in a special way. Reflect on these verses, putting them in your own words:

PSALM 73:25 _____

PSALM 34:18 _____

PSALM 51:17 _____

Having met God, we are then challenged by the same invitation Jesus gave to His disciples: "Follow Me". This "following" is a process characterized by a walk of faith and obedience. As I continue to follow Him despite life's ups and downs, gradually I am at home with Him, wherever I am. This "being at home" with God — dwelling with Him moment-by-moment — is known as "abiding with God". Intimacy or *abiding* with God is not what I do for Him or how valuable I am to Him. It is Christ Himself living in me. John chapter 15 gives a clear picture of this.

Sin can destroy intimacy and break my fellowship with God, yet it never changes my relationship. I am forever a part of the family of God. Through Christ's death on the cross and resurrection, my sin is forgiven.

Describe your fellowship with God. _____

_____

_____

How does Christ ask His disciples to stay with Him in
Luke 9:23? _____

_____

What does Christ command us in John 14:21? _____

_____

How does this apply to you today?

_____

_____

In John 15:5, Christ illustrates our relationship to Him as
that of a branch to a vine. What do you observe about this
relationship that applies to us today?

_____

_____

_____

We often think we must do something to enter into and maintain intimacy with God.
What does Christ say in the above verse? _____

_____

_____

_____

It has been said we should be characterized by the direction, not by the perfection, of
our walk. Describe the direction of your walk — toward or away from God?

_____

_____

_____

_____

IV. HOW CAN WE FIND GOD IN OUR SUFFERING?

Down in the Valley. There is a less pleasant, but equally necessary, step we take if we are to know God more deeply. We must understand how to deal with suffering. In the midst of the pain and problems of life we have the opportunity to choose how we will respond. Often it is either to persevere or get angry. A *full* definition of suffering is to persevere in the presence of pain. Too often we equate suffering only with pain. However, with perseverance comes a depth of intimacy with Him that is otherwise unavailable.

Describe the role of perseverance in the presence of pain in these passages:

ROMANS 5:1-3 _____

_____

JAMES 1:2-4 _____

_____

How does Christ help us in our suffering in these verses?

2 CORINTHIANS 1:3-5 _____

_____

1 PETER 2:20,21 _____

_____

What will God do for you as you persevere?

2 PETER 3:15 _____

_____

"God whispers to us in our pleasures, speaks in our conscience, but shouts in our pains: it is his megaphone to rouse a deaf world."

C. S. LEWIS IN *THE PROBLEM OF PAIN*

Has this been your experience? In what way? _____

_____

What role does a closely knit community of believers have as one walks through these difficult times? _____

_____

How does 1 Corinthians 12:26 apply to this subject? _____

_____

Review this chart from the book *Lifestyle Discipleship* by Jim Petersen:

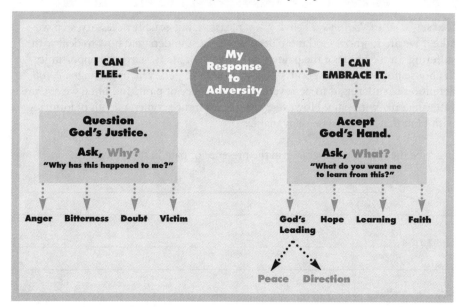

From the diagram above, what are the different choices that are available when going through suffering? What are the results of each choice? _____

_____

_____

Describe a difficulty or trial you may be going through. _____

_____

_____

How could these principles you have studied in this section apply to this? _____

_____

What else do you learn about suffering in Philippians 1:29? _____

_____

We see pain and trouble through different eyes when we realize it's part of a necessary process, and that — no matter how circumstances may appear — God has plans "too wonderful for me to know".

JEREMIAH 29:11 "For I know the plans I have for you," declares the Lord, "plans to prosper you and not to harm you, plans to give you hope and a future."

Hope and Help. How does God minister to us when we are hurting? (ISAIAH 40:27-31)

_____

_____

According to that verse, what kind of people have their strength renewed? _____

_____

God has designed us to know Him, deeply and meaningfully. It takes a heart that is hungry and thirsty to get to know God above everything else in life. We usually don't experience that kind of exclusive hunger and thirst for God until we realize our power-lessness, brokenness and need for God. We don't usually realize we are powerless until we go through experiences that are beyond our control and our ability to resolve. Regular prayer, disciplined study of God's Word, and lessons in the difficult school of experience are the means by which God forms us into His own image. No shortcuts are on the map of God's kingdom.

But the destination is worth the journey! There is no true joy in life apart from the knowledge of God.

What thought or insight impacted you from this chapter on "Intimacy with God"?

_____

_____

_____

_____

_____

_____

Scripture Memory Verse:

5 Intimacy with God   NIV

ISAIAH 41:10
So do not fear, for I am with you; do not be dismayed, for I am your God. I will strengthen you and help you; I will uphold you with my righteous right hand.

ISAIAH 41:10

For Further Study: *Experiencing God*, Henry Blackaby
Making Sense Out of Suffering, Peter Kreeft
The Loveliness of Christ, Samuel Rutherford
(Canon Press, Moscow, Idaho)

NOTES

_____

_____

_____

_____

_____

_____

_____

_____

_____

_____

_____

_____

_____

_____

_____

_____

_____

_____

_____

_____

_____

_____

REFLECTIONS

"Jesus did not come to explain away suffering or remove it. He came to fill it with His presence."

PAUL CLAUDEL

6 Knowing God's Will

THERE'S NO MAP, BUT I'D BE HAPPY TO DRIVE THE CAR!

That's What They Say:

What is God's will for my life? — is not *the right question. I think the right question is: What is God's will? Once I know God's will, then I can adjust my life to Him. In other words, what is it that God is purposing where I am. Once I know what God is doing, then I know what I need to do. The focus needs to be on* God, not *my life!*
HENRY BLACKABY'S EXPERIENCING GOD

I seek at the beginning to get my heart into such a state that it has no will of its own in regard to a given matter. Nine-tenths of the trouble with people generally is just here. Nine-tenths of the difficulties are overcome when our hearts are ready to do the knowledge of what His will is. GEORGE MUELLER, PASTOR IN ENGLAND, 19TH CENTURY

Not my will, but Thy will be done. JESUS CHRIST

WARMUP

The Cosmic Roadmap. If you could directly ask God one question, what would it be? _____

_____

Chances are, it would relate to His will for your future, possibly in the area of vocation. Wouldn't life be simple if a letter would flutter down from the skies, with a specific, non-negotiable answer written for us?

We all know life isn't like that. How can we discern God's will? Is there a secret formula? The Bible has much to say on the area of guidance.

THE BIG PICTURE.

In this chapter we'll discuss four areas:

I. Does God have a plan?
II. Knowing God's will for everyone
III. Discerning God's will
IV. Keeping the channels clear

I. DOES GOD HAVE A PLAN?

Today many believe that time and events are basically meaningless and random. Humanity is on its own in a world that, if not hostile, is at least ambivalent. Let's survey the Bible's view.

Read Ephesians 1:10-11. Summarize the relationship between God and history described here. _____

_____

What place do people play in God's scheme, according to this passage? _____

_____

Now back up to Ephesians 1:4. How long has God known you? _____

_____

How do you feel about the fact that God knew you and had plans for you long before you were born? _____

_____

_____

But what about the small things? Read Matthew 6:25-34 and comment on God and "details". _____

_____

Why is it important for God to have a plan? _____

_____

In summary, God works His purpose out through history. This includes events great and small, and certainly the issues of our lives. Note that whenever His purposes are discussed in Scripture, His love is generally mentioned. The two are inseparable.

II. KNOWING GOD'S WILL FOR EVERYONE

Many people think of God's will as a great mystery. Actually, most of the answers are already available in your Bible. If we could master those commands we already have, we would be left with few questions about what else we should be doing.

Always Do This. The following can be called "no-brainers". That is, it is always God's will that you...

1 THESSALONIANS 4:3-5 _____

1 THESSALONIANS 5:18 _____

1 PETER 2:15 _____

Some other of God's objectives for you are as clearly stated in the following verses. God wants you to...

MATTHEW 6:33   treat others like you would like to be treated

MATTHEW 7:12   seek God's kingdom and His righteousness first

MATTHEW 28:19-20   be holy in the way you live

1 PETER 1:15   be honest

ROMANS 12:17   win and disciple others for Christ

As you can imagine, this list could go on for many pages. When in doubt about God's will, you can be sure that it will never depart from what He has already commanded. God never changes.

More often than we might think, our questions about the will of God will end right here. The more we dig into the Bible and learn what He has already said, the fewer questions we are likely to have.

"Earnest Christians seeking guidance often go wrong. Why is this? Often the reason is that their notion of the nature and method of divine guidance is distorted....They overlook the guidance that is ready at hand and lay themselves open to all sorts of delusions. Their basic mistake is to think of guidance as essentially inward prompting by the Holy Spirit, apart from the written Word."

J. I. PACKER, IN KNOWING GOD

III. DISCERNING GOD'S WILL

Not So Fast! The previous section leaves a note of uncertainty — this sounds great, but what about career questions? What about deciding whom to marry, or whether to buy a house?

Indeed, these are complex questions about which we must seek God's will.

A key verse: Proverbs 3:5-6. What insights for discovering God's will is revealed here?

_____

_____

_____

_____

What was the psalmist's attitude in Psalm 40:8? What seems to have enhanced his desire?

_____

_____

_____

_____

> "The will of God is not like a magic package let down from heaven by a string... The will of God is far more like a scroll that unrolls every day... The will of God is something to be discerned and to be lived out every day of our lives. It is not something to be grasped as a package once for all. Our call, therefore, is basically not to follow a plan or a blueprint, or to go to a place or take up a work, but rather to follow the Lord Jesus Christ."
>
> PAUL LITTLE,
> *AFFIRMING THE WILL OF GOD*

Cross-Examination. As you seek God's will in a decision, it is natural to ask yourself a few questions about the options. Principles from Scripture will guide you. Match the principle with the Scripture verse:

1 CORINTHIANS 6:12	stay away from sexual sins; this sin is against my own body
1 CORINTHIANS 6:18-20	whatever you eat or drink, do to God's glory
1 CORINTHIANS 8:9	everything is permissible, but everything is not beneficial
1 CORINTHIANS 10:31	my exercise of freedom can injure weaker people

Read Psalm 25:4-5. Write your own version of David's prayer, making reference to a question you have in your own life at present. Offer what you write as a prayer to God.

_____

_____

_____

_____

On One Condition. Romans 12:2 sets a condition for our being able to "test and approve what God's will is". Explain in your own words what that condition is.

_____

_____

_____

_____

Who will personally help you make your decision about God's will? (JOHN 16:13)

_____

_____

What difficult principle is dealt with in Psalm 27:14? Do you find this challenging?

_____

_____

What further strategy is found in Proverbs 19:20? _____

_____

God certainly uses Christians to help in the guidance of other Christians. Through your experiences, you will be given insight to pass on to younger Christians. List the name of two or three wise, mature Christians who know you well enough to give good advice.

_____

_____

What promise, found in Psalm 32:8, should we remember? _____

_____

George Mueller, a 19th century English pastor, well-known for his walk of faith, wrote how he maintained a "heart" relationship with God and how he learned to discern God's voice. These principles sum up what we have studied in this lesson.

1. I seek at the beginning to get my heart into such a state that it has no will of its own in regard to a given matter. Nine-tenths of the trouble with people generally is just here. Nine-tenths of the difficulties are overcome when our hearts are ready to do the knowledge of what His will is.

2. Having done this, I do not leave the result to feeling or simple impression. If so, I make myself liable to great delusions.

3. I seek the Will of the Spirit of God through, or in connection with, the Word of God. The Spirit and the Word must be combined. If I look to the Spirit alone without the Word, I lay myself open to great delusions also. If the Holy Ghost guides us at all, He will do it according to the Scriptures and never contrary to them.

4. Next I take into account providential circumstances. These often plainly indicate God's Will in connection with His Word and Spirit.

5. I ask God in prayer to reveal His Will to me aright.

6. Thus, (1) through prayer to God, (2) the study of the Word, and (3) reflection, I come to a deliberate judgment according to the best of my ability and knowledge, and if my mind is thus at peace, and continues so after two or three more petitions, I proceed accordingly.

George Mueller's *Answers to Prayer from George Mueller's Narratives*, Brooks, A.E.C, Moody Press

What is your reaction to George Mueller's approach to discerning God's voice?

_____

_____

What significance for your own life does this have? _____

_____

_____

_____

IV. KEEPING THE CHANNELS CLEAR

We study God's Word; we pray and seek the leadership of the Spirit, as well as that of wise Christians. We can then be certain God will guide us in His time and way. But to keep in close touch with God and discern His will properly, you must keep the channels of communication clear.

How does the Psalmist keep the channels clear, in Psalm 143:8? _____

_____

Why do you think a regular daily time with God might be helpful? _____

_____

_____

What do you feel is the importance of 1 John 1:9 in keeping clear communication with God? _____

_____

_____

How can the warning in Hebrews 10:25 be an appropriate safeguard? _____

_____

_____

_____

Preventive Maintenance. An ounce of prevention is truly worth a pound of cure: seeking God daily, dealing immediately with sin, and staying accountable to other Christians — do these things and you can't venture far from the will of God. Remember that He never seeks to hide it from you; He's eager to be a part of your life and reveal Himself to you.

The following chart gives you some questions that might help you in making a particular decision.

Scriptural Guidelines	YES	NO
Is my heart's desire *"Not my will, but Yours be done?"*		
Will I love God and others more as a result of this?		
Am I waiting patiently on God to teach me and reveal Himself to me through His Word?		
Am I being completely honest with myself (and others I have sought for counsel)?		
Will this increase my desire to win and disciple others for Christ?		
Will it help me *"be holy as He is holy"?*		
Will it help me grow in my relationship to Christ and in my training to become more effective for Him?		
Am I obeying the verses that clearly state God's will, i.e. "In everything give thanks…" "Avoid sexual immorality…" "By doing good, silencing the ignorance of foolish men…"		
Has God shown me His will in some other area that I need to obey before deciding this?		
Has God shown me recently in His Word something that relates to this? What?		
Have I prayed about it?		
Have I sought counsel from other mature Christians?		
Do I have inner spiritual peace about making this decision?		

Caution: Do not use this as a "checklist" to find God's will. These are only principles to help you examine your heart and evaluate where you are in the process of seeking Him first and foremost in every area of your life, not just in trying to make a decision.

What is a decision that you are facing (job, financial, relational)?

_____

_____

_____

Other helpful exercises: Make a list of the pros and cons of this decision; then make a list of alternative choices and the pros and cons for each.

PRO	CON

ALTERNATIVE	PRO	CON

What has impacted your life from this lesson?

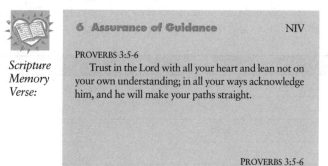

Scripture Memory Verse:

6 Assurance of Guidance   NIV

PROVERBS 3:5-6

Trust in the Lord with all your heart and lean not on your own understanding; in all your ways acknowledge him, and he will make your paths straight.

PROVERBS 3:5-6

NOTES

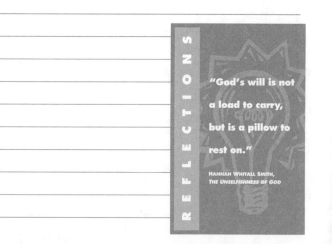

"God's will is not a load to carry, but is a pillow to rest on."

HANNAH WHITALL SMITH, *THE UNSELFISHNESS OF GOD*

4 Transformed, not conformed NIV

ROMANS 12:1-2

Therefore, I urge you, brothers, in view of God's mercy, to offer your bodies as living sacrifices, holy and pleasing to God — this is your spiritual act of worship. Do not conform any longer to the pattern of this world, but be transformed by the renewing of your mind. Then you will be able to test and approve what God's will is — his good, pleasing and perfect will.

ROMANS 12:1-2

5 Intimacy with God NIV

ISAIAH 41:10

So do not fear, for I am with you; do not be dismayed, for I am your God. I will strengthen you and help you; I will uphold you with my righteous right hand.

ISAIAH 41:10

6 Assurance of Guidance NIV

PROVERBS 3:5-6

Trust in the Lord with all your heart and lean not on your own understanding; in all your ways acknowledge him, and he will make your paths straight.

PROVERBS 3:5-6

1 The Word of God NIV

2 TIMOTHY 3:16-17

All Scripture is God-breathed and is useful for teaching, rebuking, correcting and training in righteousness, so that the man of God may be thoroughly equipped for every good work.

2 TIMOTHY 3:16-17

2 Assurance of Answered Prayer NIV

PHILIPPIANS 4:6-7

Do not be anxious about anything, but in everything, by prayer and petition, with thanksgiving, present your requests to God. And the peace of God, which transcends all understanding, will guard your hearts and your minds in Christ Jesus.

PHILIPPIANS 4:6-7

3 Christ and the Church NIV

COLOSSIANS 1:18

And he is the head of the body, the church; he is the beginning and the firstborn from among the dead, so that in everything he might have the supremacy.

COLOSSIANS 1:18

TEN MOST-WANTED

1.
2.
3.
4.
5.
6.
7.
8.
9.
10.

I will faithfully pray for the salvation of the above and will attempt to reach them for Christ through personal witness and various outreach efforts.

"The earnest prayer of a righteous man has great effect." JAMES 5:16

1 The Word of God KJV

2 TIMOTHY 3:16-17

All scripture is given by inspiration of God, and is profitable for doctrine, for reproof, for correction, for instruction in righteousness: That the man of God may be perfect, throughly furnished unto all good works.

2 TIMOTHY 3:16-17

2 Assurance of Answered Prayer KJV

PHILIPPIANS 4:6-7

Be careful for nothing; but in every thing by prayer and supplication with thanksgiving let your requests be made known unto God. And the peace of God, which passeth all understanding, shall keep your hearts and minds through Christ Jesus.

PHILIPPIANS 4:6-7

3 Christ and the Church KJV

COLOSSIANS 1:18

And he is the head of the body, the church: who is the beginning, the firstborn from the dead; that in all things he might have the preeminence.

COLOSSIANS 1:18

4 Transformed, not conformed KJV

ROMANS 12:1-2

I beseech you therefore, brethren, by the mercies of God, that ye present your bodies a living sacrifice, holy, acceptable unto God, which is your reasonable service. And be not conformed to this world: but be ye transformed by the renewing of your mind, that ye may prove what is that good, and acceptable, and perfect, will of God.

ROMANS 12:1-2

5 Intimacy with God KJV

ISAIAH 41:10

Fear thou not; for I am with thee: be not dismayed; for I am thy God: I will strengthen thee; yea, I will help thee; yea, I will uphold thee with the right hand of my righteousness.

ISAIAH 41:10

6 Assurance of Guidance KJV

PROVERBS 3:5-6

Trust in the Lord with all thine heart; and lean not unto thine own understanding. In all thy ways acknowledge him, and he shall direct thy paths.

PROVERBS 3:5-6